W9-BJK-995

HORSES SET I

THOROUGHBRED HORSES

BreAnn Rumsch
ABDO Publishing Company

visit us at
www.abdopublishing.com

Published by ABDO Publishing Company, 8000 West 78th Street, Edina, Minnesota 55439. Copyright © 2011 by Abdo Consulting Group, Inc. International copyrights reserved in all countries. No part of this book may be reproduced in any form without written permission from the publisher. The Checkerboard Library™ is a trademark and logo of ABDO Publishing Company.

Printed in the United States of America, North Mankato, Minnesota.
042010
092010

 PRINTED ON RECYCLED PAPER

Cover Photo: Corbis
Interior Photos: Alamy pp. 11, 15; AP Images p. 13; Corbis p. 5;
    David Burton / FLPA / Minden Pictures p. 17; Getty Images p. 20; iStockphoto p. 7;
    Photolibrary pp. 9, 19

Editor: Tamara L. Britton
Art Direction & Cover Design: Neil Klinepier

Library of Congress Cataloging-in-Publication Data

Rumsch, BreAnn, 1981-
  Thoroughbred horses / BreAnn Rumsch.
      p. cm. -- (Horses)
  Includes index.
  ISBN 978-1-61613-423-5
  1. Thoroughbred horse--Juvenile literature. I. Title.
  SF293.T5R86 2011
  636.1'32--dc22
                                    2010010566

CONTENTS

Where Thoroughbreds Came From

Horses have been used to explore vast new lands and plow endless fields. Today, these mammals also provide us with entertainment and excitement.

The horse's earliest ancestor lived about 60 million years ago. It is called eohippus. From this small creature, many horse **breeds** developed. They all belong to the family **Equidae**.

The Thoroughbred horse is an impressive breed that started more than 300 years ago. Several Englishmen brought three Arabian horses to England from the Middle East. The first Thoroughbreds descended from these Arabians.

The Darley Arabian, the Byerly Turk, and the Godolphin Arabian laid the foundation for the Thoroughbred breed.

In 1730, the Thoroughbred horse arrived in North America. Then in 1894, the Jockey Club formed. This group maintains the American Stud Book. It documents all Thoroughbred **breeding** in North America.

WHAT THOROUGHBREDS LOOK LIKE

The Thoroughbred is a widely recognized horse **breed**. This beautiful animal takes many of its features from its Arabian relatives. The Thoroughbred has widely spaced, intelligent eyes and a delicate head. Its neck is long and graceful.

However, the Thoroughbred horse is a racing machine! It has a slim body with a short, curved back. Powerful muscles command all four of the horse's long legs.

Thoroughbred horses weigh about 1,000 pounds (450 kg). On average, they stand about 16 hands high. One hand equals four inches (10 cm). This measurement is taken from the ground up to the **withers**.

The word **thoroughbred** *is sometimes used to refer to any animal of pure breeding. But, the Thoroughbred horse is a specific breed.*

WHAT MAKES THOROUGHBREDS SPECIAL

For more than 300 years, **breeders** have been perfecting the Thoroughbred's racing qualities. Today, these horses combine amazing speed and great strength. Secretariat and Man o' War are among the most famous Thoroughbred racehorses.

Today, races vary from five-eighths to one and one-half miles (1 to 2.4 km) long. During a race, Thoroughbreds can gallop at more than 40 miles per hour (64 km/h). A Thoroughbred's single stride can cover more than 20 feet (6 m) of ground!

Thoroughbreds are more than just powerful racehorses. These animals also excel at jumping and other sports. Thoroughbreds are even **crossbred** with other horse types to improve those **breeds**.

A Thoroughbred's hooves endure incredible pounding as the horse speeds across the ground.

COLOR

At the racetrack, many fans identify a favorite Thoroughbred by the **jockey**'s colorful uniform. That may be because the horses often display similar coat colors. Common colors include bay, chestnut, gray, and black.

Bay horses have light to dark reddish brown coats with black points. Points are the horse's legs, mane, and tail. Chestnut horses have brown coats and points.

Gray horses are born with dark hair that often turns white with age. Black horses have all black coats and points. Yet, they can still have white markings.

Markings are solid white patches of hair found on the head and the legs. They can be seen on any

Thoroughbred horse. Common head markings are a star, a stripe, a **blaze**, a **snip**, and a **bald face**. Leg markings include ankles, socks, and stockings.

Markings are important features breeders use to identify individual Thoroughbreds.

CARE

A racing Thoroughbred works very hard. So, it needs a comfortable place to rest. The horse's stall should offer plenty of clean bedding and fresh air.

A veterinarian should examine your horse at least once each year. He or she can prevent illness by **deworming** the horse and giving it **vaccines**. The veterinarian can also float the horse's teeth if they are uneven. This involves filing any sharp points to prevent chewing problems.

A farrier can trim your Thoroughbred's hooves and replace worn horseshoes as needed. Racing horseshoes are lightweight. They may wear out after just a few races. You should clean your horse's hooves daily with a hoof pick.

After a hard workout, your Thoroughbred will need to be cooled down. Walk the horse to help it

slowly adjust from work to rest. Then, wash away any sweat to make your horse more comfortable.

Grooming your Thoroughbred's coat is an important final step. Use a rubber currycomb and a body brush to remove dirt and dust. Then, rub your horse's coat with a clean cloth to add shine.

FEEDING

A horse's diet affects its performance. So, take care when feeding a racehorse. Thoroughbreds usually eat a combination of grass, hay, and grain. Types of hay include dried grasses and alfalfa. Oats, barley, and corn are common types of grain.

Horses need a lot of food each day to fuel their powerful bodies! They may eat 20 pounds (9 kg) of hay. They can also eat between 4 and 12 quarts (3.8 and 11.4 L) of grains. The exact amount depends on a horse's size and age. It also varies with the horse's level of work or exercise.

Supplements can add to the horse's health. For example, a salt lick replaces salt lost while sweating. And, cod-liver oil provides the horse with many vitamins.

Your horse may drink between 10 and 12 gallons (38 and 45 L) of water daily. So fresh, clean water should always be available. However, giving your Thoroughbred water right after exercise could cause illness.

Hay provides the bulk of the horse's food. It can be fed from a hay net.

THINGS THOROUGHBREDS NEED

To be ridden properly, a Thoroughbred horse needs special equipment called tack. Tack includes a saddle, a saddle pad, and a bridle. A saddle protects a horse's back and makes riding easier. A saddle pad lays underneath the saddle and absorbs sweat.

Riders can use Western or English saddles. Ranchers and trail riders prefer to use Western saddles. English saddles are lighter than Western saddles. So, they are better for racing and jumping.

Every rider uses a bridle to control his or her horse. Most bridles consist of a headstall, a bit, and reins. The headstall fits on the Thoroughbred's head. It attaches to the bit, which fits in the horse's mouth. Reins attach to the bit and are held by the rider.

Tack must fit a Thoroughbred well to prevent discomfort. After riding, always clean the tack to protect your horse from germs.

A Thoroughbred's racing saddle weighs much less than a normal English saddle. In fact, it is barely there!

How Thoroughbreds Grow

Breeding Thoroughbred horses is serious business. Breeders are careful to mate the best parents they can. An adult female horse is called a mare. The male parent is called a stallion. After they mate, the mare may become **pregnant**.

About 11 months later, the mare gives birth to a baby Thoroughbred. The newborn is called a foal. It takes its first wobbly steps soon after birth. In just hours, the foal can already run.

A foal also quickly learns to nurse. After about six months, the foal is **weaned**. However, some racehorses are weaned after just three or four months.

Foals born closest to January 1 have the most time to mature.

American **breeders** want their Thoroughbred foals born as soon after January 1 as possible. That is because on the following January 1, they officially become **yearlings**. Most horses go on to live for 20 to 30 years.

TRAINING

Before a horse learns to race, it must learn some basic lessons. A foal first learns to trust humans. Next, it accepts wearing a halter on its head. This piece of tack makes a horse easier to handle. The foal also learns to walk beside a person.

A Thoroughbred horse begins training for its racing career as a **yearling**. At this young age, it learns to follow commands, change pace, wear tack, and be ridden. Then, it trains on a racetrack with a **jockey**.

As a two-year-old, a Thoroughbred horse can enter its first race. Racing events are exciting and competitive.

For example, only three-year-old Thoroughbreds can compete to win the **Triple Crown**. This means a horse gets just one chance to become the winner. Through 2009, only 11 horses have achieved this feat.

By the time Thoroughbreds are five years old, many are retired from racing. However, they can be retrained for other purposes. These beautiful horses continue to thrill horse lovers every day!

A well-trained Thoroughbred can be a perfect horse for many activities!

GLOSSARY

bald face - a white, wide marking covering most of an animal's face.

blaze - a usually white, broad stripe down the center of an animal's face.

breed - a group of animals sharing the same ancestors and appearance. A breeder is a person who raises animals. Raising animals is often called breeding them.

crossbreed - to mate two different breeds of the same species.

deworm - to rid of worms.

Equidae (EEK-wuh-dee) - the scientific name for the family of mammals that includes horses, zebras, and donkeys.

jockey - a person who rides a horse in a race.

pregnant - having one or more babies growing within the body.

snip - a white marking between a horse's nostrils.

supplement - something added to make up for a shortage of substances necessary to health.

Triple Crown - a title earned by a horse for winning three specific classic horse races. In U.S. horse racing, these are the Kentucky Derby, the Preakness Stakes, and the Belmont Stakes.

vaccine (vak-SEEN) - a shot given to prevent illness or disease.

wean - to accustom an animal to eating food other than its mother's milk.

withers - the highest part of a horse's or other animal's back.

yearling - a racehorse from January 1 through December 31 of the year following its birth.

WEB SITES

To learn more about Thoroughbred horses, visit ABDO Publishing Company on the World Wide Web at **www.abdopublishing.com**. Web sites about Thoroughbreds are featured on our Book Links page. These links are routinely monitored and updated to provide the most current information available.

INDEX